Merr~

It ~~xxxxx~~ ~~xxxxx~~ f~.

our love and best
Wishes always —
aunt Laura — monty

# The Carols
# of Christmas

I heard the bells on Christmas day
Their old familiar carols play,
And wild and sweet the words repeat
Of peace on earth, good will to men.

Till, ringing, singing on its way,
The world revolved from night to day;
A voice, a chime, a chant sublime,
Of peace on earth, good will to men!

IDEALS PUBLICATIONS INCORPORATED
Nashville, Tennessee

## PHOTOGRAPHS

ISBN 0-8249-4054-7
Published by Ideals Publications Incorporated, 565 Marriott Drive, Nashville, Tennessee, 37214.

Publisher, Patricia A. Pingry; Editor, Nancy J. Skarmeas; Book Designer, Patrick T. McRae; Editorial Assistant, Laura Matter

Watercolor Border Design by Susan Harrison

# Contents

# The Night of Nights

And it came to pass in those days, that there
went out a decree from Caesar Augustus,
that all the world should be taxed. . . . And Joseph
also went up from Galilee,

out of the city of Nazareth, into Judea,
unto the city of David, which is called Bethlehem . . .
To be taxed with Mary
his espoused wife, being great with child.

Luke 2: 1, 4, 5

Led by the light of faith serenely beaming,
With glowing hearts by His cradle we stand.
So led by light of a star sweetly gleaming,
Here came the wise men from the Orient land.
The King of Kings lay in a lowly manger,
In all our trials born to be our friend.
He knows our need,
To our weakness is no stranger.
Behold your King! before Him lowly bend!
Behold your King! your King! before Him bend!

Truly He taught us to love one another;
His law is love, and His gospel is peace.
Chains shall He break, for the slave is our brother,
And in His name all oppression shall cease.
Sweet hymns of joy in grateful chorus raise we,
Let all within us praise His holy name.
Christ is the Lord!
Then ever, ever praise we;
His power and glory evermore proclaim!
His power and glory evermore proclaim!

# O Holy Night

**O** *Holy Night* is one of the most solemn and beautiful Christmas songs ever written, yet it met with strong disapproval from church authorities at the time of its composition. One French bishop even derided the song for its "lack of musical taste and total absence of the spirit of religion."

Such disapproval was not new to the song's composer, Adolphe Charles Adam, a nineteenth-century Frenchman best known for his opera *Giselle*. As a boy growing up in Paris, Adam desired nothing more than the chance to study music at the Paris Conservatory. His father, a well-known pianist and an instructor at the Conservatory, believed that the life of a musician was a difficult one not suitable for his son. The elder Adam resisted his son's desire to devote his life to music and insisted instead that he study law. Adolphe persevered, however, and secretly taught himself to play the piano. So impressed was his father by Adolphe's commitment and talent that he eventually relented his pressure and allowed young Adolphe to enter the Conservatory. In very little time Adolphe Adam became an accomplished composer and, later, a teacher.

Adam wrote the music for the song we know as *O Holy Night* and asked his close friend, the French poet Cappeau de Roquemaure, to write a set of lyrics. They called their collaboration *Cantique de Noel*. The words we sing today in America come from the pen of a clergyman and music scholar named John Sullivan Dwight. Dwight's English translation transformed *Cantique de Noel* into *O Holy Night,* one of the most elegant and moving of all Christmas solo songs, a song that is, contrary to the opinion of some nineteenth-century French bishops, full of the "spirit of religion."

# It Came upon a Midnight Clear

Edmund H. Sears

Richard S. Willis

It came up-on the mid-night clear, That glo-rious song of old, From an-gels bend - ing near the earth, To touch their harps of gold. "Peace on the earth, Good will to men, From heav'n's all gra - cious King." The world in sol - emn still-ness lay, To hear the an - gels sing.

Still through the cloven skies they come
With peaceful wings unfurled;
And still their heavenly music floats
O'er all the weary world.
Above its sad and lowly plains,
They bend on hovering wing;
And ever o'er its Babel sounds
The blessed angels sing.

Yet with the woes of sin and strife
The world has suffered long;
Beneath the angel-strain have rolled
Two thousand years of wrong.
And man, at war with man, hears not
The love song which they bring.
Oh, hush the noise, ye men of strife,
And hear the angels sing.

O ye, beneath life's crushing load,
Whose forms are bending low,
Who toil along the climbing way
With painful steps and slow,
Look now! for glad and golden hours
Come swiftly on the wing.
O rest beneath the weary road
And hear the angels sing.

For lo! the days are hast'ning on,
By prophets seen of old,
When with the ever circling years
Shall come the time foretold.
When the new heav'n and earth shall own
The Prince of Peace their King,
And the whole world send back the song
Which now the angels sing.

# It Came upon a Midnight Clear

Edmund Hamilton Sears wrote the words to our beloved Christmas hymn, *It Came upon a Midnight Clear,* as he sat in his study in Wayland, Massachusetts, one cold, snowy December day in 1849. Sears was a devout and serious man. Upon graduation from Harvard Divinity School, Sears turned down offers from large, urban churches and chose instead to live a quiet life in a small country parish. Blessed neither by a powerful speaking voice nor by robust health, Sears was also extremely shy. In Wayland he was able to serve God in the quiet and thoughtful way that suited him best.

Sears had much to think about as Christmas approached in 1849. It was a time of great unrest in the nation. The question of slavery had begun to divide Americans, and the prospect of civil war loomed darkly on the horizon. As he looked out upon the peaceful, snowy December landscape, Edmund Sears' mind was full of the troubles of the nation as well as the miracle of Christmas. The words that he wrote that day expressed his fervent belief that the message of the Christmas angels—"peace on earth, good will to men"—could be heard even in the most troubled times.

It is hard to believe that the music that accompanies Sears' lyrics was not written with his words in mind, but it was not. The tune is the creation of Richard Willis, a composer and music journalist from New York. Willis composed the music—a tune he called *Study No. 23*—the same year that Sears wrote the words; but it was several years before another man joined the music of Willis with the words of Edmund Sears to create *It Came upon a Midnight Clear.*

Oliver Wendell Holmes once called *It Came upon a Midnight Clear* "one of the most beautiful hymns ever written." Yet the song's appeal goes beyond the beauty of its melody or its poetry to its powerful message of hope. In 1849 Sears' words reminded Americans to "hear the angels sing" during their darkest hours. Today we too listen to Sears' song and take comfort in the timeless message of the Christmas angels.

# Silent Night

Rev. Joseph Mohr–1792-1848

Franz Gruber–1787-1863

Si - lent night, Ho - ly night; All is calm, All is bright,

Round yon Vir - gin Moth - er and Child!

Ho-ly In-fant so ten-der and mild, Sleep in heav-en-ly

peace __, Sleep __ in heav - en - ly peace. __

Silent night, holy night;
Shepherds quake at the sight.
Glories stream from heaven afar;
Heav'nly hosts sing Alleluia.
Christ the Saviour is born;
Christ the Saviour is born.

Silent night, holy night;
Son of God, love's pure light;
Radiant beams from Thy holy face,
With the dawn of redeeming grace.
Jesus, Lord, at Thy birth;
Jesus, Lord, at Thy birth.

Silent night, holy night,
Wondrous Star, lend thy light;
With the angels let us sing,
Alleluia to our King;
Christ the Saviour is born,
Christ the Saviour is born.

# Silent Night

In 1839 a touring group of Austrian singers came to the United States and sang a simple, gentle Christmas hymn they called *Stille nacht*, or *Silent Night*. The song, whose authors were at the time unknown, immediately became a cherished part of American Christmas tradition.

It would be another fifteen years before the mystery behind *Silent Night* began to unfold. In 1854, due to conflicting claims of authorship, the German government conducted an investigation into the song's origins. The investigation led to the tiny village of Oberndorf, high in the Austrian Alps. On Christmas Eve Day 1818, Joseph Mohr, a young priest at Oberndorf's Church of St. Nicholas, wrote a song he hoped would be played at that evening's midnight service. Since the church organ was broken, Mohr asked his friend schoolmaster Franz Gruber to compose a tune for his song that could be played on guitar. Gruber worked quickly; at midnight on that Christmas Eve in the church of St. Nicholas, the people of Oberndorf heard the very first performance of *Stille nacht*, sung by two voices accompanied by a pair of guitars.

Mohr and Gruber were pleased with their song, but thought nothing more of it. Christmas passed, and their work at the church occupied their minds. They did not know that the repairman who had come after Christmas to work on their organ had seen a copy of *Stille nacht* and played it as he worked. The organ repairman remembered the song when he returned to his native village of Zillerthal, and he passed it on to the Strasser Sisters, a touring singing group. Before long, the Strasser Sisters were singing *Stille nacht* across Germany, the rest of Europe, and the world.

Mohr and Gruber never knew the fame their song achieved. They were not officially recognized as the song's authors until the investigation of 1854, six years after the death of Joseph Mohr. For them life in Oberndorf had continued much as it had before Christmas Eve 1818, yet from their tiny village in an isolated corner of the Austrian Alps, these two devout men had touched the hearts of Christians across the globe with their simple musical vision of the Nativity.

# The World Waits

And there were in the
same country shepherds abiding
in the field, keeping watch over
their flock by night. And, lo,
the angel of the Lord came
upon them, and the glory
of the Lord shone round
about them: and they were sore
afraid. And the angel said unto
them, Fear not: for, behold,
I bring you good tidings
of great joy, which shall
be to all people.

Luke 2: 8-10

# As Lately We Watched

Anonymous

Austrian Carol

As late-ly we watch'd o'er our fields thro' the

night, a star there was seen of such glo-ri-ous light;

All thro' the night,___ an-gels did sing,___ In

ca-rols so sweet of the birth of a King.

A King of such beauty was ne'er before seen,
And Mary his mother so like to a queen.
Blessed be the hour, welcome the morn,
For Christ our dear Saviour on earth now is born.

His throne is a manger, His court is a loft,
But troops of bright angels, in lays sweet and soft,
Him they proclaim, our Christ by name,
And earth, sky, and air straight are filled with his fame.

Then, shepherds, be joyful; salute your new King;
Let hills and dales ring to the song that ye sing.
Blessed be the hour; welcome the morn;
For Christ our dear Saviour on earth now is born.

# As Lately We Watched

Like so many of our favorite Christmas carols, *As Lately We Watched* tells the story of the shepherds who, in the fields near Bethlehem, heard the angels' proclamation that the Saviour had come. These songs are so wonderfully appealing because they tell of the inclusion of the common people—as well as the kings—in the night of Christ's birth and in his message of redemption.

The origins of *As Lately We Watched* are a complete mystery. Most sources call it an Austrian traditional carol, but nothing more is known. Its tune bears a striking resemblance to the music for *We Wish You a Merry Christmas*, but no connection between the two songs can be proven. It is most likely the work of an inspired poet who, contemplating the words of the Gospels and the meaning of Jesus Christ in his or her own life, felt a special bond with those long-ago shepherds who were invited to witness a miracle in the manger. The words which that anonymous poet wrote remain with us today and have lost none of their meaning through the years. *As Lately We Watched,* no matter what its origins, gives wonderful voice to our joy and wonder at Christmastime.

# The First Noel

The First Noel has ancient and uncertain origins. The song first appeared in print as *The First Nowell* in a book published in England in 1833 by William Sandys called *Christmas Carols Ancient and Modern*. Sandys gave no particular source for the song; and despite the efforts of historians, no precise story has been verified.

One popular theory is that *The First Noel* originated as part of a thirteenth- or fourteenth-century miracle play. Miracle, or mystery, plays were dramatizations of Biblical stories that grew out of the liturgical dialogue carried on between priest and congregation in the medieval church. The word "miracle" here refers to Christ's redemption of mankind. The text of this dialogue, which came from Biblical and apocryphal sources, eventually grew so long and involved that it was taken out of the service and performed separately in the churchyard, and later on the streets of the village. The performances became a favorite form of public entertainment, especially at holiday time. Miracle plays were a way for the common, uneducated people to participate in religious holiday celebration. Many music authorities believe that the roots of *The First Noel* lie in one such play.

It is unlikely that this theory will ever be proven or disproved; and in truth, it has not been a matter of concern to the generations who have come to love this song as an expression of their Christmas joy. In William Sandys' book, *The First Nowell* carried the credit line "traditional," which is a convenient way of saying that for as long as anyone can remember, *The First Noel* has been a part of Christmas.

# Once in Royal David's City

In her travels throughout Ireland with her Anglican bishop husband, Cecil Frances Alexander spoke openly and forcefully about God to both the converted and the wayward, but she saved her special attention and energy for the children. Alexander loved to write hymns and poems for children. Her hope was that her words could make the lessons of the Bible more understandable and more meaningful to the youngest of God's faithful. *Once in Royal David's City* is probably the best known of all her hymns. It appeared for the first time in the collection *Hymns for Little Children* in 1848. The song's simple lyrics—which tell the story of the Nativity with an emphasis on the fact that Jesus too was once a small child—hold a timeless appeal for parents and children alike.

Mrs. Alexander never met the composer who set her words to music, but one can imagine that she would have heartily approved of Henry Gauntlett, a prolific composer who is said to have written over ten thousand hymn tunes.

As a young boy, Henry Gauntlett showed a faith and determination beyond his years. Entranced by the music of the church organ, Henry pleaded with his father to allow him to take lessons. His father finally gave in, but he did not take Henry seriously until, on a playful challenge from his father, the young boy copied the music of over one thousand works of the great composers. From that day on, nobody took Henry Gauntlett's devotion to church music lightly. At the age of nine, he became the organist at his church in Olney, England; and for the remainder of his life he composed and played church music. We are fortunate that, out of his vast catalogue of works, Henry Gauntlett found a tune to fit the charming text of Mrs. Alexander's *Once in Royal David's City.*

# O Little Town of Bethlehem

In the year 1868 Phillips Brooks found the memory of a recent Christmastime trip to the Holy Land "still singing in [his] soul." As Christmas approached once more, Brooks sat down to put his thoughts on paper. He arose after writing one of the most cherished Christmas carols in any language, *O Little Town of Bethlehem*.

Brooks wrote the song for a children's Christmas pageant at Philadelphia's Holy Trinity Church, where he was pastor. It was the parishioners at Holy Trinity who had paid for his trip to the Holy Land as a gesture of thanks and appreciation for his enthusiastic and devoted service. At the age of thirty Brooks had experienced what many Christians only dream about: he had spent Christmas in Bethlehem, visited the fields where the shepherds first heard the word that the Saviour had come, and attended midnight services at the Church of the Nativity, built on the traditional site of the manger where Jesus was born. *O Little Town of Bethlehem* was Brooks' attempt to make his experience in Bethlehem real for the children of his Philadelphia parish. In its sweet and comforting lines can be found something akin to the peace and inspiration Brooks must have felt as he looked upon the site of Jesus' birth almost two thousand years after the first Christmas Eve.

The tune for *O Little Town of Bethlehem* is the work of Lewis Redner, who was the organist and Sunday school superintendent at Holy Trinity and a close friend of Phillips Brooks. Redner always spoke of the tune as a gift from heaven, for he went to sleep on the Saturday night before it was to be performed without a single note written. He later reported that, during the night, the melody came to him like an "angel strain." The next day Redner taught his tune and Brooks' lyrics to the children, and *O Little Town of Bethlehem* made its debut.

# The Gift Is Given

And so it was, that, while they were there, the days were accomplished that she should be delivered. And she brought forth her firstborn son, and wrapped him in swaddling clothes, and laid him in a manger; because there was no room for them in the inn.

Luke 2: 6-7

# Away in a Manger

Martin Luther–1483–1546

Carl Mueller

A - way in a man - ger, no crib for a bed, the

lit - tle Lord Je - sus lay down His sweet head. The

stars in the sky__ looked down where He lay, the

lit - tle Lord Je - sus, a - sleep on the hay.

The cattle are lowing; the poor baby wakes;
But little Lord Jesus no crying He makes.
I love Thee, Lord Jesus. Look down from the sky
And stay by my cradle till morning is nigh.

Be near me, Lord Jesus, I ask Thee to stay
Close by me forever and love me, I pray.
Bless all the dear children in Thy tender care
And take us to heaven to live with Thee there.

# Away in a Manger

**P**opular legend has it that *Away in a Manger* was the song German religious reformer Martin Luther sang to his children as he rocked them in their cradles at Christmastime. Charming as it is, however, to imagine a great man such as Luther in an act of fatherly affection, the legend has no basis in fact. *Away in a Manger* is of American origin and first appeared in the mid-nineteenth century, more than three hundred years after the time of Martin Luther.

The legend of Martin Luther and *Away in a Manger* was the creation of a man named James R. Murray who, in 1887, published a book he entitled *Dainty Songs for Little Lads and Lasses.* The book included a song called *Luther's Cradle Hymn,* which Murray reported was "composed by Martin Luther for his children and still sung by German mothers to their little ones." This song was what we now know as *Away in a Manger.*

It is impossible to say where Murray got his story or why he told it as truth. Regardless of his motive, however, subsequent editions of Christmas songs included *Luther's Cradle Hymn* with Martin Luther given as the author.

In 1954 an American, Richard S. Hall, discovered that the verses printed in Murray's book in 1887 had appeared some twenty years earlier in *The Little Children's Book,* published by German Lutherans living in Pennsylvania. The Lutherans published the song without an acknowledged author or composer. Hall also discovered that *Away in a Manger* was virtually unknown in Germany before the publication of Murray's book. It seems that neither Martin Luther nor German mothers were singing *Luther's Cradle Hymn* to their children.

Richard Hall disproved the legend of Martin Luther and *Away in a Manger,* but he was unable to discover the song's true author or composer. Today we label it "traditional" and gladly accept it as a universal Christmas lullaby, a sweet, gentle song that tells the Christmas story on its most basic, human level: a mother, a child, and the miracle of new life.

# What Child Is This?

The music for the lovely Christmas carol *What Child Is This?* has a long and varied history. Legend has it that the tune was originally written by Henry VIII as a dance song for his daughter, the future Queen Elizabeth I. The first public record of the tune dates to 1580, when a man named Richard Jones registered the song as *Greene Sleves*. Jones' lyrics were distinctly lacking in Christian message and bear no relation to the song we know today. Only ten days later, another version of the song was entered upon the public register; this time the song, also titled *Greene Sleves*, was described as "moralised to the Scripture, declaring the manifold benefits and blessings of God." The song was on the right track, at least, but still had a long way to go. For the next three hundred years, *Greensleeves*, as it became known, remained popular in England. Shakespeare mentioned it twice in *The Merry Wives of Windsor*, and it served for a time as the regular background music at the hanging of British traitors.

The song's modern history began in 1865 when the poet William Chatterton Dix wrote and published "The Manger Throne," a long poem about the Nativity. Three stanzas of Dix's poem became the verses of *What Child Is This?* The tune *Greensleeves* that we sing with Dix's words was arranged by Englishman John Stainer, an organist at the University of Oxford and at St. Paul's Cathedral in London.

The tune *Greensleeves* has continued its long and varied life apart from Dix's lyrics. It has been the theme song for radio and television programs and has also—in keeping with its history—often been the musical setting of very unreligious verses. Yet the combination of *Greensleeves* and the words of William Chatterton Dix seems most fitting and has proven most lasting. At Christmastime, when we sing *What Child Is This?*, the words and music sound as though they were written solely for each other.

# O Come, O Come, Emmanuel

The words to *O Come, O Come, Emmanuel* are ancient, dating back to medieval days when they were sung in Latin throughout Advent by the most pious monks. The song is an example of plainsong, a type of liturgical music sung in unison without harmony, strict meter, or accompaniment. At vespers on the evening of December 17, the abbot would rise before his brethren and intone the first verse of *O Come, O Come, Emmanuel*. On each succeeding night through the twenty-third of the month a solitary monk would sing a new verse. The combined verses were known as *The Seven O's*. Despite the fact that to our modern ears plainsong sounds rather solemn, *The Seven O's* were a joyous tribute to the Saviour.

The English translation of the Latin verses comes from an Englishman named John Neale. In the nineteenth century, an unidentified musician set Neale's words, with the addition of the refrain "Rejoice! Rejoice! Emmanuel shall come to thee, O Israel," to a more modern sounding tune. Today, *O Come, O Come, Emmanuel* can be sung with harmony and accompaniment, but it has not lost the free flowing feeling or the heartfelt emotion that it expressed in medieval days, when pious monks made *The Seven O's* a centerpiece of their Advent celebration.

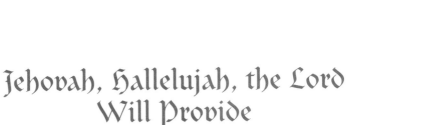

# Jehovah, Hallelujah, the Lord Will Provide

*Jehovah, Hallelujah, the Lord Will Provide* is an American folk carol for Christmas, born in South Carolina as part of the Christmas Eve Watch Night service. The song addresses Mary's worry that there is no place for her to rest in Bethlehem and gives the joyous answer that for all our needs, the Lord will provide.

Watch Night began just after supper on Christmas Eve, when the community would gather at the church for a night of song and prayer. Alternating between the minister's sermon and group song, the congregation would tell the story of Christmas, from the journey to Bethlehem to the birth of the Baby to visits of the shepherds and the three Wisemen to a final great celebration of the message of Christ's arrival. Many of the folk songs sung on Watch Night were created by individual congregations, and most underwent adaptations from year to year and group to group. *Jehovah, Hallelujah, the Lord Will Provide* is one that has gained more general popularity and a standardized form.

The appeal of this charming Christmas carol, like the appeal of all lasting folk songs, is in its universal and simple message. There is no greater joy or comfort to any of us than the knowledge that no matter what befalls us as faithful Christians, the Lord in His infinite wisdom and power will provide for us all.

# The Friendly Beasts

One of the most beloved Christmas legends tells of how the animals around the manger received the gift of speech on the night Jesus was born. With their newfound voices, the animals paid tribute to the tiny infant and the message of peace and goodwill that he brought to the world. The appeal of this legend is easy to understand. Not only does it speak of the miraculous powers of the newborn infant, but it proves the all inclusiveness of his love and his message: even the simple beasts of the world are touched by his presence.

*The Friendly Beasts* is an English carol from the twelfth century that, in keeping with the legend of the night the animals talked, gives voice to several of the residents of the Bethlehem stable where Christ was born: the donkey who carried Mary, the cow who gave up her stall for the mother and child, the sheep whose fleece provided warmth for the infant, the dove whose sweet voice sang the child to sleep, and the camel who carried one of the Wisemen to the manger. Each speaks proudly and reverently of his contribution to the most wonderful night and the most blessed child. The tune for the animals' song comes from France, where it was written some time during the Middle Ages.

*The Friendly Beasts* is a song for children. Their natural love for animals and willingness to accept the extraordinary makes it easy for them to hear the newfound voices of the inhabitants of the stable. It is also a song for all Christians, a song to remind us that Christ's love touches all of God's creatures and that all who come with open hearts and open minds are welcome at the manger in Bethlehem at Christmastime and throughout the year.

# Go Tell It on the Mountain

Go Tell It on the Mountain is a true American folk song, a rousing spiritual that celebrates the birth of Jesus Christ the Saviour. The song came to the attention of the world in 1879, when the Fisk University Jubilee Singers traveled throughout the United States and Europe performing the traditional music of African-Americans. The aim of the Singers was to raise money for scholarships; in the process they also raised awareness by exposing listeners, including Queen Victoria of England, to the beauty and emotion of Go Tell It on the Mountain and countless other spirituals.

The origins of Go Tell It on the Mountain are uncertain. Like most spirituals it evolved through group singing, and no one author or composer can be given credit. The text takes inspiration from the Sermon on the Mount and urges the faithful to climb to the highest mountaintops to proclaim the news of Jesus' birth. This wonderful news offers hope to every believing Christian, no matter how low or downtrodden or disheartened. A song for Christmas, or for any time when the light of faith is needed to brighten the day, Go Tell It on the Mountain is a powerful tribute to its unknown first author and to the generations of American Christians who have helped shape this and other spirituals by joining their voices in tribute to Jesus Christ.

# The Announcement Made

For unto you is born this day
in the city of David a Saviour,
which is Christ the Lord.
And this shall be a sign
unto you; Ye shall find
the babe wrapped in
swaddling clothes,
lying in a manger.

Luke 2: 11-12

# There's a Star in the Sky!

Josiah G. Holland, 1819-1881

Karl P. Harrington, 1861-1953

There's a song in the air! There's a star in the sky!

There's a moth-er's deep prayer And a Ba-by's low cry!

And the star rains its fire while the beau-ti-ful sing,

For the man-ger of Beth-le-hem cra-dles a King!

There's a tumult of joy
O'er the wonderful birth,
For the Virgin's sweet Child
Is the Lord of the earth.
Ay! the star rains its fire and the choirs sing,
For the manger in Bethlehem cradles a King.

In the light of that star
Lie the ages impearled;
And that song from afar
Has swept over the world.
Every hearth is aflame, and the choirs sing
In the homes of the nations that Jesus is King.

We rejoice in the light,
And we echo the song
That comes down through the night
From the heavenly throng.
Ay! we list to the lovely message they bring,
And we greet in His cradle our Saviour and King.

# There's a Star in the Sky!

The American Christmas carol *There's a Star in the Sky!* trumpets the news of Jesus' birth across the years and in every corner of the globe. Also known as *There's a Song in the Air!*, the song is a proclamation of Christmas joy.

The author of the carol, Josiah Gilbert Holland, was a man of many talents and interests who came to writing rather late in life. As a young man in his native western Massachusetts, Holland had tried his hand at teaching, photography, medicine, and journalism before, in 1881 at the age of sixty-two, he settled into a career as editor of *Scribner's Monthly* magazine. *There's a Star in the Sky!* had appeared two years earlier in Holland's *Complete Poetical Writings*. It was this widely read book that secured his future as a poet.

Holland's poem is sung to a tune written by Karl Pomeroy Harrington, a composer from Somersworth, New Hampshire. Harrington, a professor of Latin, wrote the music before the publication of Holland's poem. On a trip around the world years later, he heard his tune as the accompaniment to Holland's words sung by children in Japan, China, and India. Harrington was touched by the universal appeal of his music and pleasantly surprised by the beauty of its pairing with Holland's text.

It is not surprising, however, that *There's a Star in the Sky!* has universal appeal among Christians, for the song describes not only the wonderful presence of Jesus in the manger at Bethlehem, but also his continuing presence in the everyday lives of believers in every corner of the world.

# Angels We Have Heard on High

French legend has it that shepherds in the country's southern hills watching their flocks on Christmas Eve would call to each other across the fields and hills, singing the words "*gloria in excelsis Deo*," which is Latin for "glory to God in the highest." The shepherds' song, an imitation of the song of the angels as they announced the birth of Christ on the first Christmas Eve, came from a second-century Latin chorale made popular when Pope Telesphorus, the pontiff from 125 to 136, ordained that "*gloria in excelsis Deo*" be sung at midnight mass each Christmas Eve.

In France in 1855, the Latin refrain sung by the shepherds was joined to the text and tune we sing today to become *Angels We Have Heard on High*. The verses come from a French carol called *Les anges dans nos campagnes* and the music from a popular French song of the day.

Many people today associate this lovely carol with London's Westminster Abbey, where it was introduced to English audiences by the Westminster Abbey Choir. Following their example, choirs across England and the United States have adopted *Angels We Have Heard on High* as a regular part of their Christmas repertoire. Its festive pace and inspirational refrain make it the perfect expression of the joyous, miraculous message of Christmas; and its history as a shepherd's carol make it a lovely choice for group singing.

# Hark! The Herald Angels Sing

Neither the composer nor the author of *Hark! The Herald Angels Sing* ever heard the song played or sung. In fact, by the time William H. Cummings united the music of Felix Mendelssohn with the words of Charles Wesley, the former had been dead for seven years, and the latter for sixty-seven. Nonetheless, these two men—Wesley, a prolific English hymn writer, and Mendelssohn, a brilliant German composer—receive credit for the song which became one of the most popular and widely sung Christmas carols in America and Great Britain.

Mendelssohn might have been surprised had he lived to see what Cummings did with his music. The tune which we all know as *Hark! The Herald Angels Sing* is part of a choral work called *For a Tercentenary of the Invention of the Art of Printing,* which Mendelssohn wrote to celebrate the achievements of Johannes Gutenberg, the German who invented movable type. Mendelssohn had been particularly pleased with his tune and imagined that with less esoteric lyrics it might become popular. But he was adamant about one thing: his tune, he stated on several occasions, "will never do to sacred words."

Wesley, who along with his brother John founded the Methodist church, published four thousand hymns in his lifetime and left manuscripts for two thousand more at his death. It is unlikely that he had great expectations for the text that Cummings selected to pair with Mendelssohn's music. It is also unlikely that he would be entirely satisfied with the many alterations made in his text to facilitate the adaptation.

It is useless, however, to speculate on what the two men might have thought about the course their words and music took. Their collaboration is part of history now, and the song that resulted has been part of Christmas for generations. *Hark! The Herald Angels Sing* is not only a joyous, reverent celebration of the Christmas miracle, but one that seems to be a permanent part of the way we mark the season.

# Angels, from the Realms of Glory

**A**ngels, from the Realms of Glory is one of more than four hundred hymns written by a devout Scottish newspaper editor and poetry teacher named James Montgomery. Montgomery was a divinity student when his interest in poetry led him into the publishing business, but he never lost the strong faith that had guided him toward the ministry. He once remarked that each of his hymns "was born of a distinct Christian experience."

Montgomery was known in his hometown of late eighteenth-century Sheffield, England, as an outspoken liberal. On two occasions, local authorities imprisoned him for views expressed in his newspaper. While in prison he wrote a book he called *Prison Amusements*. This strong-minded text only served to increase his reputation as a man of unbending faith and principles. Upon his release, Montgomery found that his newspaper, *Iris*, was more popular than ever. It was in *Iris*, on Christmas Eve of 1816, that *Angels, from the Realms of Glory* first appeared in print.

It was not until thirteen years after Montgomery's death, however, that a London composer, inspired by the words of the hymn, wrote a vigorous, cheerful tune to accompany them. That composer was Henry Smart, who, like Montgomery, had started down one career path only to have his passion for another calling divert him. For Smart, who had studied as a young man to become a lawyer, it was music that changed his direction. He devoted the latter part of his life to composing and organ playing. Smart's most lasting musical achievement is the music for Montgomery's hymn, which he committed to paper by dictation after illness had taken his sight. The elegant tune, called *Regent Square* after a large Presbyterian church in London, is a wonderful setting for the triumphant message of Montgomery's lyrics.

# Everywhere, Everywhere, Christmas Tonight

Phillips Brooks

Lewis H. Redner

Christ - mas in lands of the fir tree and pine,

Christ - mas in lands of the palm tree and vine,

Christ - mas where snow peaks stand sol - emn and white,

Christ - mas where corn - fields lie sun - ny and bright,

Ev - 'ry - where, ev - 'ry - where, Christ - mas to - night.

Christmas where children are hopeful and gay,
Christmas where old men are patient and gray,
Christmas where peace, like a dove in its flight,
Broods o'er brave men in the thick of the fight—
Everywhere, everywhere, Christmas tonight!

For the Christ Child who comes is the Master of all,
No palace too great and no cottage too small;
The angels who welcome Him sing from the height,
"In the city of David, a King in His might."
Everywhere, everywhere, Christmas tonight!

Then let every heart keep its Christmas within,
Christ's pity for sorrow, Christ's hatred for sin,
Christ's care for the weakest, Christ's courage for right,
Christ's dread of the darkness, Christ's love of the light.
Everywhere, everywhere, Christmas tonight!

So all the stars of the midnight which compass us round
Shall see a strange glory and hear a strange sound,
And cry, "Look! the earth is aflame with delight:
O sons of the morning, rejoice at the sight."
Everywhere, everywhere, Christmas tonight!

# Everywhere, Everywhere, Christmas Tonight

Everywhere, Everywhere, Christmas Tonight is the lesser known of the two great Christmas carols to come out of the collaboration of Phillips Brooks and Lewis Redner in the mid-nineteenth century. Brooks and Redner served together at Holy Trinity Church in Philadelphia, the former as pastor and the latter as organist. Their other Christmas carol is *O Little Town of Bethlehem*.

*Everywhere, Everywhere, Christmas Tonight* is a wonderfully accurate representation of the personality and beliefs of Phillips Brooks. Its verses celebrate the universality of the Christmas spirit just as Brooks devoted his life to uniting people through Christian faith. Pastor Brooks was motivated by a deep and warm love for Jesus Christ, a love which he also felt for all God's sons and daughters. At a time when many church leaders were tempted to intellectualize religion, Brooks was passionately evangelical. He went on from Philadelphia to become pastor at Trinity Church in Boston and later Episcopal Bishop of Massachusetts; but, no matter what his position, it was everyday contact with his parishioners—and the chance to deepen their faith by his own words and ministry—that appealed to Phillips Brooks. Upon Brooks' death a young girl was heard to remark, "How happy the angels will be." This was a fitting tribute to a man who brought the joyous light of faith to countless lives and who continues to spread the good word a century after his death with the lovely *Everywhere, Everywhere, Christmas Tonight*.

# COME . . .

And it came to pass, as the angels were gone away from them into heaven, the shepherds said one to another, Let us now go even unto Bethlehem, and see this thing which is come to pass, which the Lord hath made known unto us. And they came with haste, and found Mary, and Joseph, and the babe lying in a manger.

Luke 2: 15-16

# We Three Kings of Orient Are

Rev. John H. Hopkins—1820–1891

We three Kings of O - ri - ent are; Bear-ing gifts we tra-verse a - far, Field and foun-tain, moor and moun-tain, fol-low-ing yon-der star. O__ star of won-der, star of night, star with roy-al beau-ty bright, west-ward lead-ing still pro - ceed - ing, guide us to thy per - fect light.

Born a King on Bethlehem's plain,
Gold I bring to crown Him again,
King forever, ceasing never,
Over us all to reign.

Star of wonder, star of night,
Star with royal beauty bright,
Westward leading, still proceeding,
Guide us to thy perfect light.

Frankincense to offer have I;
Incense owns a Deity nigh;
Prayer and praising, all men raising,
Worship Him God most high.

Star of wonder, star of night,
Star with royal beauty bright,
Westward leading, still proceeding,
Guide us to thy perfect light.

Myrrh is mine; its bitter perfume
Breathes a life of gathering gloom:
Sorrowing, sighing, bleeding, dying,
Sealed in the stone cold tomb.

Star of wonder, star of night,
Star with royal beauty bright,
Westward leading, still proceeding,
Guide us to thy perfect light.

Glorious now behold Him arise,
King and God and Sacrifice.
Alleluia, Alleluia,
Earth to heaven replies.

Star of wonder, star of night,
Star with royal beauty bright,
Westward leading, still proceeding,
Guide us to thy perfect light.

# We Three Kings of Orient Are

John Henry Hopkins was a man of many talents. The son of the Bishop of Vermont, Hopkins wrote poetry, designed stained glass windows, taught and wrote music, and served as rector in several churches. In 1857 Hopkins was the church music teacher at the General Theological Seminary in New York City. It was his job to plan and produce the annual Christmas pageant. Hopkins wrote several new songs for that year's pageant, one of which he called *We Three Kings of Orient Are*.

Nearly one hundred and fifty years later, Hopkins's song is still a Christmastime favorite. Its popularity is due in great part, undoubtedly, to its wonderful musical composition. *We Three Kings of Orient Are* lends itself to choir singing or Christmas pageants, with the three parts of the kings perfectly suited for the beautiful voices of young boys. The song is also enjoyed for its unique perspective on the Nativity. Thanks to Hopkins's song, Melchior, Caspar, and Balthazar—the three kings of legend who traveled across the desert to look upon the baby Jesus and bestow upon him the precious gifts of gold, frankincense, and myrrh—are familiar characters to children at Christmastime. The example of their humility and reverence at the manger is repeated every time the lovely lines of *We Three Kings of Orient Are* are sung.

Joy to the World

# While Shepherds Watched Their Flocks by Night

In the mid-nineteenth century it was not unheard of for American composers to attach the name of George Frederic Handel to their own compositions in hopes of gaining a wider audience. The German-born Handel's immensely popular *Messiah* had made his name synonymous with great religious music, and lesser known and more meagerly talented composers were eager to share in his fame. Another tactic was to take a piece of one of Handel's works and adapt it to some new text. Either way, the name of Handel attached to a piece of music attracted attention.

Richard Storrs Willis, an editor of music publications who wrote the tune for *It Came upon a Midnight Clear*, must have been aware of the power of Handel's name when he chose a section of the German composer's opera *Cyrus* as the musical setting for a text he selected from Nicholas Brady and Nahum Tate's *New Version of the Psalms*. The text, called "Song of Angels," was a close retelling of the section of Luke 2 that begins "And there were in the same country shepherds abiding in the field, keeping watch over their flock by night." The result of Willis's combination of the inspirational music of Handel and the Biblical paraphrase of Tate and Brady was *While Shepherds Watched Their Flocks by Night*.

Willis's impeccable selection of sources paid off. The text was so close to the Bible and the music so perfectly pedigreed that *While Shepherd's Watched Their Flocks by Night* was one of only six secular hymns that church authorities of the day allowed their congregations to sing during the service. Today it remains a favorite of church singers looking for a musical expression of the miracle of Jesus' birth.

# O Come, All Ye Faithful

Latin Hymn Tr. By
Canon Frederick Oakeley 1802-1880

J. F. Wade 1711-1786

O come, all ye faith-ful, Joy-ful and tri-um-phant, O

come __ ye, O come ye to Beth - le - hem;

Come and be - hold _Him, Born the King of An - gels; O

come, let us a - dore Him, O come, let us a - dore Him, O

come, let us a - dore Him, __ Christ __ the Lord.

Sing, choirs of angels,
Sing in exultation;
Sing, all ye citizens of heav'n above;
Glory to God in the highest.

O come, let us adore Him;
O come, let us adore Him;
O come, let us adore Him,
Christ the Lord.

Yea, Lord, we greet Thee,
Born this happy morning;
Jesus, to Thee be glory giv'n,
Word of the Father, now in flesh appearing.

O come, let us adore Him;
O come, let us adore Him;
O come, let us adore Him,
Christ the Lord.

# O Come, All Ye Faithful

Frederick Oakley, an English clergyman in the nineteenth century, loved church singing. He believed that hymns possessed a unique power to unite and inspire a congregation. He also believed that hymns must have verses of a literary quality to match their high purpose in the church. Oakley devoted a great amount of time to searching for songs worthy of the voices of his congregation. He found one such work in the Latin hymn *Adeste fideles*. Oakley translated the beautiful, solemn Latin verses into an equally moving English hymn and presented to his parish—and to Christians throughout the world—the beloved *O Come, All Ye Faithful*.

There is a bit of controversy as to the authorship of the original Latin text of *O Come, All Ye Faithful*. The manuscript that Oakley translated bore the name of John Francis Wade as author. Wade, an Englishman living in France in a community of Roman Catholic exiles, made his living copying and selling music. Many believe that *Adeste fideles* was one of Wade's copies rather than his original work. There is some evidence that *Adeste fideles* was known in France before Wade's day, which would support the theory that he only discovered and copied the work; but no definitive answer has been reached. What is known is that the music is the work of the English composer John Reading; also known is that the song lived up to Frederick Oakley's expectations and has become one of the most widely sung Christmas hymns of all time, both in its original Latin, and in the equally lovely English translation.

# Rise Up, Shepherd, and Follow

The traditional American spiritual, *Rise Up, Shepherd, and Follow*, recalls the form of an old European shepherd carol. Like shepherds calling to one another from their lonely hilltops, the song alternates the lines of the singer with a group refrain as the news of the birth in a Bethlehem manger is spread across the countryside.

A true spiritual, *Rise Up, Shepherd, and Follow*, has no recognized author or composer. The song's roots are in the early nineteenth century when African-Americans turned to Christianity to lead them through the darkness of slavery. To them, there was no more wonderful story to retell than that of the birth of Jesus. The song remains popular today at Christmastime as a reminder to us all to heed the message of the Christmas angels and turn our minds and hearts to the manger in Bethlehem and the Baby born within.

American soprano Dorothy Maynor introduced *Rise Up, Shepherd, and Follow* and other spirituals to the general American public. Maynor, the founder of the Harlem School of Music, sang with the Boston Symphony and toured throughout the United States and Europe. She always included the spirituals of her American ancestors in her concerts as a tribute to a form of music which not only represents an important piece of American heritage but has influenced countless modern composers, singers, and musical genres.

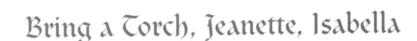

# Bring a Torch, Jeanette, Isabella

The ancient French carol *Bring a Torch, Jeanette, Isabella* first appeared in print in 1553 as part of *Cantiques de premèire advenement de Jésus-Christ*, which was the work of a French count with a special interest in Christmas music. The count's source for the song is uncertain, but most believe that the music is a French dance tune from the fourteenth century and the words an ancient folk song from either the Anjou or the Burgundy region of France.

The verses of *Bring a Torch, Jeanette, Isabella* are related to the popular medieval tradition of acting out the manger scene. The song may have originated as part of one of these informal productions which were quite popular in France throughout the sixteenth century. Some music authorities speculate that the particular words of this carol were inspired by a painting by Georges de La Tour, a French artist from the sixteenth century who painted a famous Nativity scene in which two young girls quietly watch the baby Jesus from the back of the stable.

Like most traditional carols, it is impossible to say just where and when *Bring a Torch, Jeanette, Isabella* was first sung. Nonetheless, it remains a favorite, particularly in France; for it has all the charm of an ancient folk song along with the timeless appeal of a common person's eyewitness view of the miracle of the Nativity.

# O Come, Little Children

Christmas is a day for children. On this day we celebrate the birth of Jesus in a Bethlehem manger almost two thousand years ago, and we teach our own children about the message of faith and hope that Jesus brought to the world. *O Come, Little Children* is a fitting song for the day. It brings the manger scene alive as it teaches children and reminds adults that there is an important place in God's world for Christians of all ages.

The song is the work of two accomplished Germans. The first, Christoph von Schmidt, was an author of books for children. His writing emphasized the importance of religion and morals. Born in 1768 and ordained a minister at the age of twenty-three, von Schmidt rose at four o'clock each morning to write for several hours before heading off to his job as the head of a school in Thannhauser, Germany. Von Schmidt gave us the simple, sweet lyrics of *O Come, Little Children*, with their invitation to the children of the world to celebrate the birth of Jesus.

The tune that so perfectly matches the spirit of von Schmidt's lyrics was written by J. A. P. Schultz. Born in 1747, Schultz was a child prodigy on the organ. At fifteen he traveled to Munich to study under Johann Kirnberger, who had studied under the guidance of the great Johann Sebastian Bach. Among his other accomplishments, Schultz served for eight years as the band director to the king of Denmark.

Christoph von Schmidt wanted nothing more in his life than to teach the children at his school and throughout the world the importance of religion in their lives. With *O Come, Little Children*, he went a long way toward that goal. He opened young eyes to the miracle in the manger and allowed them to understand that in God's world age is no barrier to true faith.

# . . . AND REJOICE

**A**nd suddenly there was with the angel a multitude of the heavenly host praising God, and saying, Glory to God in the highest, and on earth peace, good will toward men.

Luke 2: 13-14

# Joy to the World

Rev. Isaac Watts 1674-1748

George F. Handel 1685-1759

Joy to the world! the Lord is come; Let earth re-

ceive her King; Let ev'-ry__ heart __ pre-pare him

room,__ And heav'n and na-ture_sing; And_heav'n and na-ture

sing, And__heav'n and heav'n ___ and na-ture sing.

Joy to the world! The Saviour reigns;
Let men their songs employ,
While fields and floods,
Rocks, hills, and plains
Repeat the sounding joy, repeat the sounding joy,
Repeat, repeat, the sounding joy.

No more let sin and sorrow grow,
Nor thorns infest the ground;
He comes to make His blessings flow
Far as the curse is found,
Far as the curse is found,
Far as, far as the curse is found.

He rules the world with truth and grace
And makes the nations prove
The glories of His righteousness
And wonders of His love, and wonders of His love,
And wonders, wonders of His love.

O Jesulein süss

Gloria in excelsis Deo

Adeste Fideles

# Joy to the World

Isaac Watts devoted much of his life to the writing of hymns. To Watts, there was no more vital part of the church service and no better way to inspire a congregation than with a stirring hymn. Because of his high regard for hymns, Watts went to the most worthy source when working on lyrics: the Bible. In his lifetime, Isaac Watts published over six hundred hymns, a great many of which were paraphrases and interpretations of the Psalms. *Joy to the World*, included in a 1719 collection called *Psalms of David, Imitated in the Language of the New Testament*, was one of Watts's successful transformations of Psalm into hymn. Based on Psalm 98:4, which begins "Make a joyful noise unto the Lord, all the earth . . .," *Joy to the World* has been sung by church choirs and Christmas carolers for almost three hundred years.

The music for Watts's hymn is the work of an American composer named Lowell Mason. In the 1830s, Mason published a musical setting for *Joy to the World* in which he credited himself along with the great German composer Handel. To this day music scholars continue to argue about the meaning of Mason's inclusion of Handel in the credits. Some say that they have discovered a variety of musical phrases from Handel's *Messiah* in Mason's tune and that the American rightly gave credit to the German as co-composer. Others have searched in vain for pieces of the *Messiah* and come to the conclusion that *Joy to the World* was Mason's original composition and that the inclusion of Handel's name was credit for inspiration only. Regardless of the exact nature of Handel's contribution, the song is a lasting and undeniable classic and one of the most joyous and inspirational of Christmas carols.

# I Heard the Bells
# on Christmas Day

Henry Wadsworth Longfellow wrote the moving lines of *I Heard the Bells on Christmas Day* during a time of great personal crisis. The Civil War was raging, tearing the country in two. The poet's son, a lieutenant in the Army of the Potomac, had been seriously injured in battle. And on top of this, Longfellow was still grieving for his wife who had died tragically in a fire two years earlier. Despite great professional success (he was one of the most popular poets of the day), Longfellow was full of despair and loneliness as the Christmas season approached.

When he put his pen to paper to write the verses of *I Heard the Bells on Christmas Day,* Longfellow poured out this despair. As the song begins, the sound of the Christmas bells is a painful one for him. "There is no peace on earth," Longfellow claims; and there is no joy in the Christmas bells. Yet the bells persist; and as they ring out at the end of each verse, the poet's mood shifts. By the last stanza, Longfellow hears the Christmas bells ringing out their true message of hope and joy; and he confidently proclaims that because Jesus was born on Christmas Day, "peace on earth, good will toward men" is possible.

Longfellow's poem, set to music some ten years later by English organist John Baptiste Calkin, is a case study in the transforming power of faith. From the depths of his despair, the poet hears the persistent and uplifting message of the Christmas bells and finds himself and his faith renewed by the Christmas miracle. *I Heard the Bells on Christmas Day* is a record of Longfellow's experience as well as a chance for us to hear again the message of the Christmas bells.

# Good Christian Men, Rejoice

John Mason Neale, born in 1818 to an Evangelical clergyman, devoted his life from an early age to God. He studied at Cambridge, became a minister like his father, and set out to do the Lord's work. Despite his enthusiastic and willing spirit, however, John Neale's body was weak. At a premature age, failing health forced him to retire from the active ministry and seek a quieter form of service. Always interested in music and trained in ancient languages, Neale devoted his energies to translating and writing hymns.

*Good Christian Men, Rejoice* is Neale's most memorable Christmas hymn. Both words and music are based on a popular German song called *Nun singet und seid froh*—which translates as "now sing and be joyful." This song, in turn, came from a section of Johann Sebastian Bach's *Chorale Preludes*, which was inspired by a fourteenth-century hymn. Neale's version of the tune is spirited, and his lyrics are a joyful rewriting of the German.

Although John Mason Neale was unable to serve the Lord in the manner he first chose—the active ministry—it seems his failing health opened up an avenue in which he truly excelled. With the Christmas hymn *Good Christian Men, Rejoice* and his famous carol *Good King Wenceslas*, Neale not only served God and the church in his own day, but left a lasting legacy which is enjoyed each Christmastime by Christian singers across the world.

# O Sanctissima

Oh, how joy-ful-ly,__ Oh, how mer-ri-ly__
Christ-mas comes with its grace di-vine! Grace a-gain is
beam-ing Christ the world re-deem-ing:
Hail ye Christ-ians, hail the joy-ous Christ-mas time!

Day of holiness,
Peace and happiness,
Joyful, glorious Christmas Day.
Angels tell the story
Of this day of glory;
Praise Christ, our Saviour,
Born this Christmas Day.

Oh, how joyfully,
Oh, how merrily
Christmas comes with its peace divine!
Peace on earth is reigning,
Christ our peace regaining;
Hail, ye Christians,
Hail the joyous Christmastime!

Oh, how joyfully,
Oh, how merrily
Christmas comes with its life divine!
Angels high in glory,
Chant the Christmas story:
Hail, ye Christians,
Hail the joyous Christmastime!

# O Sanctissima

Known also as *O Thou Joyful Day* or *O How Joyfully*, *O Sanctissima* is based on a simple, ancient Latin prayer to the Virgin Mary. The Latin words of praise to Mary were written by, translated into English, and adapted to general praise of Christmas by an unknown author or authors. The mood of reverent, joyful wonder remains intact, however, despite the change in language and the shift in focus.

The tune for *O Sanctissima* is known simply as *The Sicilian Mariner's Hymn*. No connection to either Sicily or any mariner is apparent, although some suggest the song was originally part of an Italian opera. The text and tune appeared together for the first time around 1790, either in America or England. The song achieved great popularity after its inclusion in a book of hymns published by the English Reverend W. Tattersall called *Improved Psalmody*. The collection also included music by the great composer Haydn which put *O Sanctissima* in very prestigious company. The song's popularity is proven by eighteenth-century English broadsides which include *O Sanctissima* alongside *Adeste fideles*.

Today, the song is less well known in America, but it can still be heard in churches at Christmastime, where its reverent praise and joyful celebration of the miracle of Christmas are most at home.

# God Rest Ye Merry, Gentlemen

Old English

God rest ye mer - ry, gen-tle-men, Let noth - ing you dis-

may, Re-mem-ber Christ our Sa-vi-our Was born on Christ-mas

Day, To save us all from Sa - tan's pow'r, When

we were gone a - stray O _ tid - ings of com - fort and

joy, com - fort and joy, O tid - ings of com - fort and joy.

In Bethlehem, in Israel, this blessed Babe was born
And laid within a manger upon this blessed morn
The which His mother Mary did nothing take in scorn.

O tidings of comfort and joy, comfort and joy!
O tidings of comfort and joy.

From God our heavenly Father, a blessed angel came
And unto certain shepherds brought tidings of the same,
How that in Bethlehem was born the Son of God by name.

O tidings of comfort and joy, comfort and joy!
O tidings of comfort and joy.

The shepherds at those tidings, rejoiced much in mind,
And left their flocks afeeding, in tempest, storm, and wind,
And went to Bethlehem straitway, the Son of God to find.

O tidings of comfort and joy, comfort and joy!
O tidings of comfort and joy.

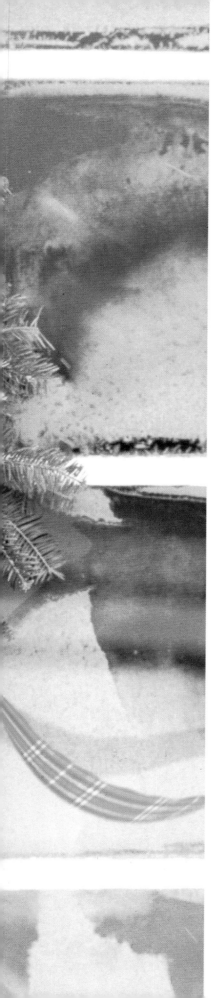

# God Rest Ye Merry, Gentlemen

**B**efore he is transformed by his night of Christmas visions, Ebeneezer Scrooge, the crusty protagonist of Charles Dickens's classic *A Christmas Carol*, hears a man full of Christmas cheer singing the lines of *God Rest Ye Merry, Gentlemen*. Scrooge, who contrary to the good advice of the song prefers to let everything "him dismay," erupts with anger and menaces the reveler with "such energy of action that the singer [flees] in terror."

Only a man as mean-spirited as Ebeneezer Scrooge could react in such a way to the timeless "tidings of comfort and joy" of *God Rest Ye Merry, Gentlemen*. First published in 1827 with no acknowledged author, this all-time favorite English Christmas carol appears to have ancient roots. Historians have learned that *God Rest Ye Merry, Gentlemen* was one of the carols sung by English *waits*—men who were paid by the government to entertain the citizenry on special occasions. The carol was also often printed on old broadsides that were handed out on the streets of London at Christmastime.

Despite their best efforts, however, music researchers can pin down no exact time of origin; *God Rest Ye Merry, Gentlemen* appears to have been a part of Christmas in England for a good long time. For centuries *God Rest Ye Merry, Gentlemen* has delivered the good news of Christ's birth with an upbeat meter and a rather solemn tone. Perhaps this dual recognition of both the joy and the reverence that we all feel at Christmas is the reason this song has remained a favorite through the years.

# The Seven Joys of Mary

Traditional

Old English

The first good joy that Ma-ry had, it was the joy of one;____ To see the bless-ed Je-sus Christ when He was first her Son.___ When He was first her Son, good Lord;_ And hap-py may we be;_Praise Fa-ther, Son, and Ho-ly Ghost to all e-ter-ni-ty.

The next good joy that Mary had,
It was the joy of two;
To see her own Son Jesus Christ
To make the lame to go.

The next good joy that Mary had,
It was the joy of three;
To see her own Son Jesus Christ
To make the blind to see.

The next good joy that Mary had,
It was the joy of four;
To see her own Son Jesus Christ
To read the Bible o'er.

The next good joy that Mary had,
It was the joy of five;
To see her own Son Jesus Christ
To bring the dead alive.

The next good joy that Mary had,
It was the joy of six;
To see her own Son  Jesus Christ
Upon the crucifix.

The next good joy that Mary had,
It was the joy of seven;
To see her own Son Jesus Christ
To wear the crown of heaven.

# The Seven Joys of Mary

The *Seven Joys of Mary* arose out of medieval devotions to the Virgin Mary. Its roots are most likely found in the Rosary, which includes among its fifteen "mysteries" the five "Joyful Mysteries." The Joyful Mysteries of the Rosary are the Annunciation to Mary by the angel Gabriel; the Visitation; the Nativity; the Presentation of Christ, when Simeon recognizes him as the Messiah; and the Finding, when Christ's mission is first publically revealed.

Through the years different miracles from Christ's life were added to the list of joys, increasing the standard five to seven. Eventually, the direct connection with the Mysteries of the Rosary was lost, and a folk song was born. The verses we know today originated in the fifteenth century in England.

The tune we sing with *The Seven Joys of Mary* is also a product of English folk tradition. Like so many other traditional tunes, it has served many purposes through the years, including that of an anthem for unemployed workers in London in the eighteenth century. It is a spirited, happy tune, fitted well to the mood of joy and celebration that is expressed by the ancient lines of *The Seven Joys of Mary*.

The Word of GOD abides

# The Traditions of Christmas

And when they had seen it, they made known abroad the saying which was told them concerning this child. And all they that heard it wondered at those things which were told them by the shepherds. . . And the shepherds returned, glorifying and praising God for all the things that they had heard and seen, as it was told unto them.

Luke 2: 17-18, 20

# O Christmas Tree

**O** *Christmas Tree*, or *O Tannenbaum*, is a German folk carol of ancient and unknown origin. Its appeal is simple to understand, for the brightly lit and decorated Christmas tree is one of the most universally cherished symbols of the Christmas season. Its evergreen branches, colorful ornaments, and bright, shining lights combine the natural, the secular, and the religious aspects of the Christmas season.

There are many legends about how the decorated evergreen became a part of Christmas. One ancient story tells that on the very first Christmas all the trees in the world celebrated Jesus' birth with their most fantastic blossoms, and from that day on, trees remained a special part of the holiday celebration. Another legend comes from Germany, where the custom of decorating the evergreen began. The story goes that the great religious reformer Martin Luther was walking in the woods on a winter's night and saw the light from the moon and the stars filtered through the branches of the evergreens. Struck by the beauty of the sight, Luther took home a fallen bough from one of the trees and thus began the custom of bringing evergreens into the home. The decorations with which we adorn our own Christmas trees are imitations of the glowing moon and sparkling stars that Luther saw in the woods that night long ago.

Regardless of the origin of the custom, however, the decorated Christmas tree is at the center of our homes and our hearts every December, and this lovely little German folk carol will forever be on our lips as we gaze with wonder at the lights and color of our Christmas tree.

# The Holly and the Ivy

Traditional

Old French Carol

The hol-ly and the i - vy, When they are both full grown, Of all the trees that are in the wood, the hol-ly bears the crown. The ris-ing of the sun, And the run - ning of the deer,__ The play - ing of the mer - ry or - gan, Sweet sing - ing of the choir.

The holly bears a blossom
As white as lily flower,
And Mary bore sweet Jesus Christ
To be our sweet Saviour.

The rising of the sun
And the running of the deer,
The playing of the merry organ,
Sweet singing in the choir.

The holly bears a berry
As red as any blood,
And Mary bore sweet Jesus Christ
To do poor sinners good.

The rising of the sun
And the running of the deer,
The playing of the merry organ,
Sweet singing in the choir.

The holly bears a prickle,
As sharp as any thorn,
And Mary bore sweet Jesus Christ
On Christmas Day in the morn.

The rising of the sun
And the running of the deer,
The playing of the merry organ,
Sweet singing in the choir.

The holly bears a bark,
As bitter as any gall,
And Mary bore sweet Jesus Christ
For to redeem us all.

The rising of the sun
And the running of the deer,
The playing of the merry organ,
Sweet singing in the choir.

# The Holly and the Ivy

The Holly and the Ivy first appeared in print in 1861, in a collection of songs published by Englishman Joshua Sylvester. Sylvester named an old English broadside, printed around 1700, as his source for the song. In truth *The Holly and the Ivy* is probably even older than that, and its symbolism dates to pre-Christian days, when holly and ivy were first connected with wintertime religious festivals.

The lively verses of *The Holly and the Ivy* carry very solemn religious symbolism relating to the birth and death of Jesus Christ. The blossoms of the holly plant— "as white as lily flower"—represent the purity of the Virgin Mary; the rich red berries are symbolic of the blood of her son Jesus; the sharp prickles on the holly stem stand for the crown of thorns that Jesus wore. In verse five, the bark of the holly—as bitter "as any gall"—signifies the bitter agony of Christ's crucifixion. The symbolic meaning of the ivy has been lost through the generations. All that is known is that in ancient England ivy was often used to represent women.

*The Holly and the Ivy* has been a part of Christmas in the English-speaking world since the time of the very first celebrations of Christ's birth, and its symbolism is a vestige of the days before the light of Christianity shone upon the world. This beloved carol is a wonderful example of how the traditions of pre-Christian antiquity, transformed by the light of Christianity, can be among our most meaningful.

# Deck the Hall

Traditional

Welsh

Deck the Hall with boughs of hol-ly, Fa la la la la, la la la la.

'Tis the sea-son to be jol-ly, Fa la la la la, la la la la.

Don we now our gay ap-par-el, Fa la la, la la la, la la la.

Troll the an-cient Yule-tide car-ol, Fa la la la la, la la la la.

See the blazing yule before us,
Fa la la la la, la la la la.

Strike the harp and join the chorus,
Fa la la la la, la la la la.

Follow me in merry measure,
Fa la la, la la la, la la la,

While I tell of Yuletide treasure
Fa la la la la, la la la la.

# Deck the Hall

In ancient Wales, Christmas was a festive family time. Preparations for the holiday centered around readying the great room of the home—decorating it with holly, ivy, and mistletoe and finding the perfect yule log for the hearth. The yule log had to be large enough to burn for the whole season and provide warmth and soft glowing light for all the holiday festivities. *Deck the Hall* is a song about these ancient Welsh holiday preparation traditions.

The tune of *Deck the Hall* is Welsh traditional, perhaps as old as the customs the song commemorates. The lyrics are more of a mystery. For a long time, it was generally agreed that the lyrics were part of the old Welsh Christmas celebrations. Some modern sources, however, credit nineteenth-century Americans with the words. Christmas as we know it in America today—the secular traditions at least—really began in the nineteenth century. Many of our holiday customs were drawn from English Victorian models, with Charles Dickens and his *A Christmas Carol* being a popular source. But anything British was considered worthy of copying. The theory is that Americans familiar with the old Welsh customs wrote the lyrics and attached to them the Welsh folk tune, creating a song with an ancient British feel to it that became an immediate American favorite.

Regardless of the true origin of the words, however, *Deck the Hall* has remained a favorite Christmas carol in America, and it has made the festive mood of those ancient Welsh Christmases, with holly and ivy and mistletoe hung from every rafter, as much a part of Christmas in America as the decorated tree.

# Here We Come a-Caroling

Traditional

English Wassail Song

Here we come a-car-ol-ing a-mong the leaves so green;___ Here we come a-wan-d'ring, so fair___ to be seen. Love and joy come to you, and to you glad Christ-mas too; And God bless you and send you a hap-py New Year, And God send you a hap-py New__ Year.

We are not daily beggars
That beg from door to door,
But we are neighbors' children
Whom you have seen before.

Love and joy come to you,
And to you glad Christmas too,
And God bless you and send you a happy New Year,
And God send you a happy New Year.

God bless the master of this house,
Likewise the mistress too,
And all the little children
That round the table go.

Love and joy come to you,
And to you glad Christmas too,
And God bless you and send you a happy New Year,
And God send you a happy New Year.

# Here We Come a-Caroling

**H**ere We Come a-Caroling has its roots in ancient England, when *wassailing* was a cherished Christmas tradition. On the nights leading up to the December holiday, men, women, and children across the countryside and in the cities would go door to door singing, hoping to be invited inside for a drink of hot spiced ale from the wassail bowl. The word *wassail* comes from the Anglo-Saxon *wase-hael*, which means "be in health." The custom of wassailing was a means of bringing best wishes to friends and neighbors and of sharing the good spirit of the Christmas season.

In London and other cities, it was most often poor and orphaned children who would go wassailing, hoping not only for a drink from the wassail bowl but also for a bit of warm-hearted Christmas generosity in the form of a penny, a hot meal, or a few moments beside the warmth of the fireplace. In the countryside, revelers often carried their wassail bowl with them as they made their rounds from farm to farm offering drinks to their neighbors. Regardless of their particular variation on the custom, the wassailers sang the lively verses of *Here We Come a-Wassailing* as they made their way through the chill winter air.

Caroling replaced wassailing in Britain during the fifteenth century, but the new tradition incorporated the song of the old, with only a slight change in the lyrics. *Here We Come a-Caroling*, sung today by happy bands of Christmas carolers, is the same song sung hundreds of years ago by English wassailers.

Today the wassail bowl is a thing of the past, but the desire to celebrate the holiday with friends and neighbors is not. When we walk through the snowy night, stop at neighbors' doors for a few spirited Christmas carols, and announce our arrival with *Here We Come a-Caroling,* we are carrying on a long tradition of Christmas generosity, fellowship, and good cheer.

# We Wish You a Merry Christmas

Traditional

English Folk Song

We wish you a mer-ry Christ-mas, we

wish you a mer-ry Christ-mas, we

wish you a mer-ry Christ-mas and a

hap-py New Year. Good ti-dings we

bring for you and your kin. We wish you a mer-ry

Christ-mas and a hap-py New Year.

Oh, bring us some figgy pudding;
Oh, bring us some figgy pudding;
Oh, bring us some figgy pudding
And a cup of good cheer.

Good tidings to you, wherever you are,
Good tidings for Christmas and a happy New Year.

We won't go until we get some;
We won't go until we get some;
We won't go until we get some,
So bring some out here.

Good tidings to you, wherever you are,
Good tidings for Christmas and a happy New Year.

We wish you a merry Christmas;
We wish you a merry Christmas;
We wish you a merry Christmas
And a happy New Year.

# We Wish You a Merry Christmas

This jolly old carol seems to have been a part of Christmas in Great Britain forever; no records exist of its origins, and no claims have been made as to the identity of its author or composer. Its lyrics suggest that it may have begun as a *waits'* carol, sung by groups of men hired by the town or city to entertain the people in the streets. Although the waits were not beggars, they often received gifts of thanks from happy listeners in the form of food or drink—thus the request for "figgy pudding" and "a cup of good cheer."

The holiday message of the English waits is now a universal Christmas greeting. All the warmth and joy and fellowship of the season is contained in the simple words uttered time after time to friends and strangers alike, in countless languages, at holiday time: "Merry Christmas!" *We Wish You a Merry Christmas* transcends time, place, religious denomination, and all other divisions of Christian people and nations. Its cheerful, upbeat lines carry the simplest and most lasting of all Christmas messages. As long as we celebrate Christmas there will be a place in our festivities for the singing of *We Wish You a Merry Christmas*.

I thought how, as the day had come,
The belfries of all Christendom
Had rolled along th' unbroken song
Of peace on earth, good will to men.

Then pealed the bells more loud and deep:
"God is not dead, nor doth He sleep;
The wrong shall fail, the right prevail,
With peace on earth, good will to men."

## INDEX

A 1
B 2
C 3
D 4
E 5
F 6
G 7
H 8
I 9
J 0